W9-BDQ-233

The Game & Fish Mastery Library

VENISON

THE GAME & FISH MASTERY LIBRARY

VENISON

By Rebecca Gray

Photography by Christopher Hirsheimer

WILLOW CREEK PRESS

Minocqua, Wisconsin

© 1998, Rebecca Gray
Photographs © Christopher Hirsheimer

Published by Willow Creek Press
P.O. Box 147
Minocqua, Wisconsin 54548

All rights reserved. No part of this book may be reproduced or transmitted in any form by any means, electronic or mechanical, including photocopying, recording, or by any information storage and retrieval system, without permission in writing from the Publisher.

Designed by Heather M. McElwain

For information on other Willow Creek titles, call 1-800-850-9453

Library of Congress Cataloging-in-Publication Data
Gray, Rebecca.
    Venison / by Rebecca Gray : photography by Christopher Hirsheimer.
        p.   cm. -- (The game & fish mastery library)
    ISBN 1-57223-185-8
    1. Cookery (Venison) I. Title. II. Series.
    TX751.G6324   1998
    641.6'91--dc21   98-34081
                                                                    CIP

Printed in Canada

TABLE OF CONTENTS

INTRODUCTION

For most of the great foods of the world no introduction is necessary. Venison is an exception. Where little explanation is needed to relay the wonderful taste of a properly aged and grilled beef steak, often as not a venison steak is viewed as "exotic" (and therefore scary?) meat left to the attentions of fancy chefs and gourmands. This is due, at least in part, to the elite status accorded venison by our state game laws. When during the turn of the century market-hunters nearly eradicated many species of wild game, laws were enacted making non-farmed meats procured for commercial purposes, venison included, illegal. This meant that for a long time the only way you were able to indulge yourself in a venison dinner was if you were fortunate enough to be asked to dine at the home of a hunter, or if you yourself hunted deer.

Making venison impossible to get at the local butcher's may have distinguished venison, but unfortunately it probably also contributed to making venison, for a time, undesirable. A hunter's repertoire usually involves finding and bringing down the animal; his or her skills may or may not include proper butchering and cooking techniques. All too many wild deer have been poorly field dressed, slung atop the hot hood of a car, "hung" in warm weather and cooked as if it were being tanned for leather. So too, the diet and age of the animal — critical elements in determining flavor — are uncontrollable factors in a wild critter. Thus the word "gamy" was born, and therefore the bad rap on many of the game meats. But it's hard to label a good food permanently with an unfavorable reputation.

I cooked my first piece of venison in the late 1960s; a white-tailed deer steak that mysteriously appeared at the Tufts University fraternity house where a boyfriend of mine lived and where I spent a lot of time. Since I was THE woman, it was assumed I knew how to cook it — quite the erroneous assumption. I recall there were deer hairs on the steak, a clear sign that the last person who'd handled the meat knew even less than I did about it. But while I carefully picked each hair off, I noticed something else: Despite whatever it had been through, it was absolutely beautiful, rich lean meat. I don't remember — probably because it was thoroughly forgettable — how I cooked it or how the venison tasted. Yes, fraternity evenings do tend toward forgetfulness, but still my curiosity and ire at the lack in my culinary knowledge had been piqued and would initiate a quest for me: How do you cook venison?

The fraternity venison also foreshadowed this now lifetime pursuit when in 1975 I married a hunter and we started our publication, *Gray's Sporting Journal*. Now I was faced not only with game in my kitchen but with editing a cooking feature for our hunting and fishing magazine. I knew I had better learn fast. I decided to query some pros: Charley Waterman, a well-known and highly regarded writer in the hunting and fishing world and Penny Reneson, the wife of one of the finest painters in the outdoor field. Both had long years of experience and continual access to game; surely they must know how to cook it. Oddly enough both had exactly the same answer to my question about what to do with venison. "We don't do much of anything — we just cook it," they both said. This was less than helpful; and it would be years before I understood what they meant by such a seemingly non-answer.

Cooking school, some research, working on the food feature in *Gray's*, drawing on a family background in the meatpacking business and, of course, trial-and-error, brought me knowledge. And perhaps not so coincidentally my own awakening seems to have mirrored a more general national interest in non-standard foods. The American attention to first French and then all European cuisine probably was initially seeded by our World War II troops experiencing firsthand other than second-generation ethnic foods. Then Julia Child would bring to the TV-watching throngs a flowering of the appreciation as well as how to and what to cook. The "what-to," being French-based and not subject to our laws, would include all game. White-tailed deer remained illegal to sell; and so market demand was in the making.

Red, fallow and Sika deer were first brought to New Zealand in the mid-1800s by European settlers, mostly English, wanting to hunt big game. The deer found ideal habitat in New Zealand and prospered; prospered to the point that their increasing population all but denuded the hills of vegetation. This caused extensive erosion, habitat loss and the near extinction of some species of ground-feeding birds. By the mid-1900s the deer were not only being hunted extensively but poisoned as pests; in 1968 nearly one million deer were killed. But then some enterprising hunters decided that instead of letting the plentiful deer carcasses just rot, they would sell them to restaurants; later, they would export venison meat. The money-making proposition caught the attention of New Zealand farmers and in the first true domestication of a wild species in over 10,000 years, the farmers captured wild deer and began propagating. Between 1970 and 1988 deer farms would grow from one to 3,500 in New Zealand, and by 1987 over 860,000 pounds of the Kiwi venison would be served in U.S. restaurants. About 85% of commercially sold venison today is still imported from New Zealand, the remaining 15% being farm-raised primarily in Texas and New York.

From 1990 to 1994 venison consumption in the U.S. doubled. Not only did the quest for European and/or unusual taste sensations drive the demand for venison, but the new emphasis on healthy, more natural foods also gave it a significant boost. Venison is high in protein, contains iron, zinc and many of the B vitamins; and it's raised naturally — absent of growth hormones, antibiotics and dyes. Plus venison is very lean. "Wild game is lean by virtue of exercise," explains Jennifer Anderson, professor of nutrition at Colorado State University's Department of Food Science and Human Nutrition. "These animals expend a tremendous amount of energy foraging and staying alive, and develop very muscular, lean tissue." There simply is no such thing as "marbled" game meat: A deer has 5% body-fat as compared to 25% for domesticated animals.

Here are some comparisons based on a serving size of 3.6 ounces:

Meat	Calories	Fat Grams	Cholesterol Milligrams	Protein Grams
Chicken (with skin)	239	17.90	83	18.2
Beef	214	9.76	92	31.0
Pork	219	10.64	101	29.0
Venison	159	3.30	66	25.0

The lower fat content and higher protein levels of wild and exotic meats makes them different to cook from their domesticated cousins, and is one reason chefs like them. As Bill Grimes of the *New York Times* wrote in a January, 1998 article, "Food is theater, after all. For audiences, what could be more exciting than seeing a new actor take the stage? For chefs, who put on the show, what could be more satisfying than exploring new creative territory?" Venison is more interesting and challenging to cook than beef or pork — requiring the choice and addition of fats, such as olive oil, cooking it hot, fast, precisely and removing it from the heat source early since the higher protein level means it will continue to cook. We've domesticated the taste right out of most of our meat, obligating the addition of salt for flavoring; with venison it's simply not necessary.

Surely it is taste, after all is said and done, that now clinches favorable repute for venison. The wonderful, intrinsic flavor of venison: It is why "nothing much" needs to be done to it and why most of the recipes in this book are simple and straightforward. "Nothing much" may sound blasé and contrary to the detailed, instructional nature of a cookbook, but don't construe this simplistic attitude for a lack of respect and attention. Venison requires not only responsibility in the field (if you are fortunate enough to procure your own wild venison) — to properly dress, transport, and butcher the venison — but, for wild and farm-raised venison alike, great care in the kitchen, too. For care is essential in the evolution and maintenance of this superior flavor. May this book help you in that pursuit, add culinary and dietary dimension to your world and make it so venison needs no further introduction.

trary to the detailed, instructional nature of a cookbook, but don't construe this simplistic attitude for

a lack of respect and attention. Venison requires not only responsibility in the field (if you are fortu-

nate enough to procure your own wild venison) — to properly dress, transport, and butcher the veni-

son — but, for wild and farm-raised venison alike, great care in the kitchen, too. For care is essential

in the evolution and maintenance of this superior flavor. May this book help you in that pursuit, add

culinary and dietary dimension to your world and make it so venison needs no further introduction.

ROASTS

SADDLE OF VENISON

We, in the U.S., have a love-hate relationship with fat: We know to avoid it for cardiovascular health reasons,
which makes lean venison desirable; but we crave the flavor of fat in our foods, particularly in meat.
This means that we add fat when cooking venison. Lard is a relatively simple fat source to use and was initially called for in this recipe.
But the pancetta (Italian bacon) now used here is a bit tastier than lard and certainly prettier.

5-6 pounds of saddle of venison
¼ cup olive oil
1 tablespoon lemon juice
Enough pancetta (5 thin slices) to cover the saddle, or use
   lard strips
1 tablespoon crushed juniper berries
1 teaspoon salt

1 onion, sliced
¼ cup red wine vinegar
5 tablespoons unsalted butter
Rind from 1 lemon
Sprinkle of flour
Salt and pepper

Combine the oil and lemon juice and rub all over the meat. Let it stand for a couple of hours. Lard with 2-inch strips in even rows with pork fat. Mix the salt and crushed juniper berries and rub all over the meat. Sauté the onion in a tablespoon of the butter and lay on the bottom of a roasting pan with the meat on top. Add the vinegar to the pan and baste the meat with the remaining butter, melted. Roast in a preheated oven at 350° for about an hour. Then sprinkle the larded meat with flour and baste again with butter. Cook until the lard is crispy.

Julienne the lemon rind and blanch for five minutes in boiling water. Combine with the juices from the roasting pan and serve on top of the sliced venison. (*Serves six*)

Venison Scallops

It is nice and consistent with culinary theory to "tie" the ingredients; here that can be done with the hazelnuts and using hazelnut oil to sauté the scallops. Hazelnut oil, like its sister walnut oil, can go rancid and should be stored in the refrigerator. Hazelnut oil is a bit healthier than walnut oil, containing lower saturated fat and higher monounsaturated fat.

2-4 whole hazelnuts (enough for 2 tablespoons finely chopped)
4 tablespoons oil
8-10 venison scallops (slice ½-inch pieces of meat from a good cut of roast, such as the tenderloin, making sure to cut across the grain)

Rind from ¼ orange
1 cup stock
¼ cup armagnac
¼ cup plus 1 tablespoon unsalted butter
Salt and pepper

Toast the whole hazelnuts in the oven till they are light brown. Wrap in a towel for 10 minutes to create steam and to loosen the skin from the nut. Rub off the skin and sauté in one tablespoon of the oil, chop fine. Remove the orange rind (making sure to get none of the white pith) from the orange with a potato peeler and julienne into slivers. Blanch for a few minutes in boiling water. Rinse, drain and reserve. Pan-fry the scalloped venison in three tablespoons olive oil for a minute or two on each side. Remove from the pan and set aside. Deglaze the pan with armagnac and then add the stock and reduce the liquid to half a cup. Whisk in the butter and season with salt and pepper. Add the nuts and orange slivers and serve over the venison scallops. (*Serves four*)

MEDALLIONS OF VENISON WITH POIVRADE SAUCE

Although roasts are usually considered the most elegant of dishes, these medallions look and taste so la-di-da
that they truly are fit for when the queen comes to visit. The best pâté de foie gras classically comes from France,
but I have found the foie gras from Quebec can equal that of their motherland.

4 small venison fillet medallions
I cup Burgundy wine
I cup water
I garlic clove, crushed
Several juniper berries, crushed
½ cup clarified butter
Pâté de foie gras (I teaspoon per medallion)

FOR THE POIVRADE SAUCE:
3 tablespoons butter
3 scallions, minced
I cup of the marinade
I small can beef bouillon
¼ teaspoon dried thyme
3 tablespoons butter, softened
3 tablespoons flour
6-8 peppercorns, crushed

Combine the wine, water, garlic and juniper berries in a sauce pan and bring to a boil, cook for five minutes. Let cool and pour over venison fillets and let marinate in the refrigerator for several hours. Remove the venison fillets, reserving the marinade, and pat dry. Now prepare the sauce by melting the butter; add the scallions and cook until tender. Stir in the marinade and bouillon and bring to a boil. Add the thyme and reduce the liquid to half. Combine the soft butter and flour, working it almost to a paste, then gradually add it to the simmering liquid, whisking it all the while until the sauce is thickened. Stir in the peppercorns. Sauté the fillets in clarified butter quickly, making sure they do not get overdone. Spread the foie gras over each venison fillet. Spoon the sauce over each fillet as it is plated. (*Serves four*)

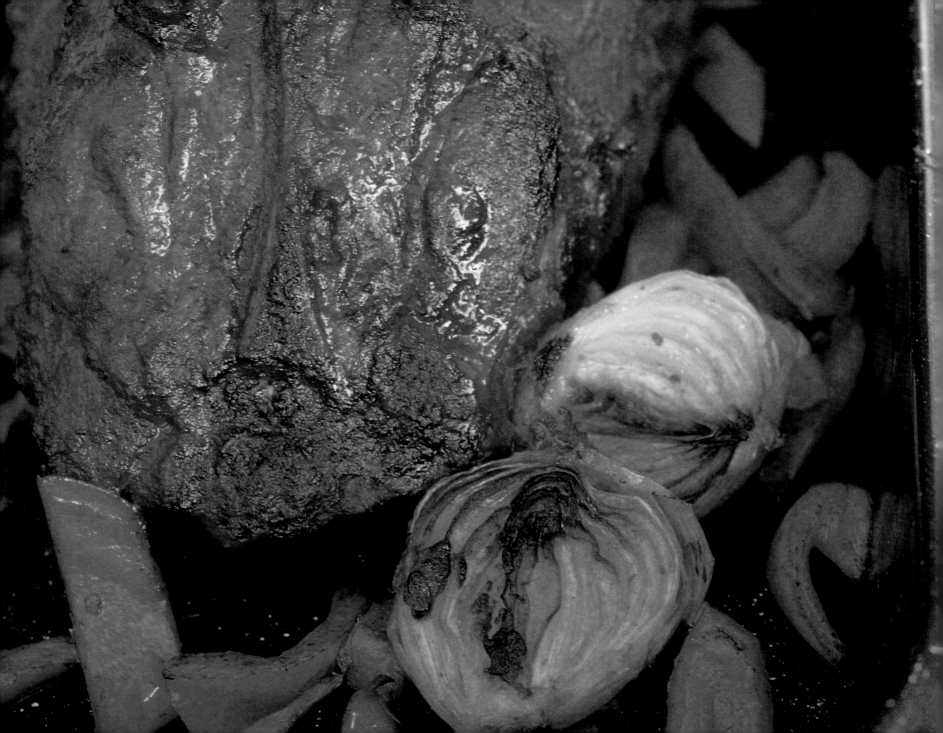

BARBECUED VENISON

Although most people think of ribs when they think of a barbecue, ribs are not a common cut of venison —
most people prefer cutting the more desirable tenderloins, crown or saddle roasts and chops when butchering the venison.
But should you crave the taste of barbecue, try this recipe. The roast can be finished on the grill for a true charcoal "barbecue" taste.

2 tablespoons butter
1 medium onion, chopped
1 bay leaf
3 tablespoons molasses
1 garlic clove, chopped
½ cup celery with leaves
¼ cup chopped green pepper
16-ounce can diced tomatoes
8-ounce can tomato sauce

2 teaspoons dry mustard
⅓ cup vinegar
½ teaspoon whole cloves
½ teaspoon whole allspice
2 slices lemon
1½ teaspoons salt
2 teaspoons Tabasco
6-7 pounds venison roast

Melt butter in saucepan. Add the garlic and onion; cook until the onion is tender. Add all the remaining ingredients, except for the venison, and simmer covered for 30 minutes. Strain, you should have about two cups of barbecue sauce. Cover the bottom and sides of a large roasting pan with aluminum foil and place a rack in it. Put the venison roast on the rack and paint the meat with barbecue sauce. Cook in a 350° oven for 15 minutes per pound, basting every 15 minutes. When done, remove and let the roast rest for 10 minutes before carving. (*Serves eight*)

Venison Roast with Golden Crust

This recipe becomes particularly elegant when using either homemade or bakery bread in making the bread crumbs.

6-8 pounds of venison roast
3 slices of crusty, dried white bread
2 garlic cloves
3 bay leaves

Salt
Fresh ground pepper
4-6 tablespoons butter, softened

Remove any fat from the venison roast. Put the bread slices, garlic and bay leaves in a blender or food processor and process until the bread is in fine crumbs and mixed thoroughly with the bay leaves and garlic. Put venison in baking pan on a rack and sprinkle with salt and pepper. Spread with the softened butter and then pat the seasoned bread crumbs all over the roast. Bake in a 350° oven for 12 minutes per pound. Let stand 15 minutes before slicing. (*Serves eight*)

Grilled Venison with Sage Leaves

The sage leaves can also be fried quickly in oil and butter and then salted and used, not as garnish, but as a wonderful taste treat.

1 loin of venison
3-4 strips bacon
1 cup unsalted butter, softened
Grated rind of 1 lemon
2 teaspoons bovril
Dash of Worcestershire sauce

2 garlic cloves
Salt and pepper
1½ tablespoons sage
Fresh sage leaves
Olive oil

Rub the venison loin with olive oil and tie on the strips of bacon. Whip the butter together with the lemon rind, Worcestershire sauce, bovril, sage, salt, and pepper. Put the garlic cloves through a press or chop very fine and add to the whipped butter mixture. Place the butter mixture on plastic wrap and shape into a log and freeze for a few hours. Preheat the grill. Grill the venison till it is rare and then let stand for 15 minutes. Slice and arrange on a platter. Season with salt and pepper and place a pat of the butter mixture on each slice. Arrange the sage leaves around the platter. (*Serves eight*)

SPIT-ROASTED VENISON

In general, I prefer venison rare; this is probably because I like all meat (except fish and chicken) rare.
This recipe in particular calls for very rare venison; so if you feel squeamish about eating game rare or generally prefer well-done meat,
then I would suggest increasing the cooking time for this and most of the other recipes in this book.

1 leg or shoulder of venison, boned, rolled and tied
   (about 4-5 pounds)
Fat salt pork for larding

FOR THE BASTING SAUCE:
½ cup oil
1 cup red wine vinegar
1 teaspoon fresh rosemary, chopped
2 garlic cloves, crushed
Salt and pepper

Combine all ingredients for the basting sauce in a blender and blend on high for a few seconds. Use salt pork to lard the venison by placing strips over the roast and then tying it. Balance the meat on the spit, making sure it turns evenly. Roast over a bed of coals, basting frequently, until the meat thermometer registers 120°, approximately 10 minutes per pound. (*Serves eight*)

VENISON WITH PORT

It is my general policy that the quality of the ingredients determines the quality of the finished recipe;
this is true of everything from herbs to chocolate. However, I believe it to be less important in the case of spirits.
The port used here need not be a thirty-year-old, fifty-dollar bottle of Portugal's finest . . . just a port.

4-5 pounds saddle of venison
Pork lard (enough to cover the saddle in 2-inch strips)
2 cups port
4 carrots
4 onions

A few parsley stems
⅔ cup unsalted butter
½ teaspoon powdered cloves
½ teaspoon cinnamon

Preheat the oven to 500°. Lard the saddle and tie with string to hold in place. Peel and chop the carrots, onions and parsley. Sauté them all in six tablespoons of the butter. Lay the vegetables on the bottom of the roasting pan and put the venison on top. Pour the port over it and roast for 10 minutes. Lower the heat to 400° and continue to cook for another half-hour or so, basting every 10 minutes. Remove the meat from the pan and skim off the fat. On top of the stove, reduce the liquid that's left to about half a cup. Add the cinnamon and cloves and whisk in the remaining butter and any juices that have exuded from the standing venison. Check the sauce for seasoning and serve over the sliced venison. (*Serves eight*)

CHRISTMAS VENISON

This roast is particularly festive because of the pretty orange rind mixed in with the compound butter.
But really venison all by its self makes for a Christmas celebration anytime.

8 pounds tenderloin rubbed with a peeled garlic clove
   and well-larded
Bunch of fresh thyme

FOR THE COMPOUND BUTTER:
¾ cup unsalted butter at room temperature
Grated rind of 1 large orange
1 small garlic clove, peeled and chopped fine
2 teaspoons chopped or crushed fennel seeds
Salt and pepper
2 tablespoons chopped parsley

Whip the butter until fluffy. Add the orange rind, fennel seeds, garlic, parsley, salt and pepper. Whip together and place on a piece of plastic wrap. Mold into a log and freeze overnight. Bring to room temperature before using. Preheat the oven to 400°. Roast the venison on a rack set on top of the fresh thyme sprigs for a nice aroma. Roast for 10 minutes per pound; remove and let rest for 15 minutes before carving. Slice, season with salt and pepper, arrange on a platter. Put a pat of the compound butter on each slice so it will melt into the meat. (*Serves ten*)

Venison Tenderloin

When cooking meat it's often recommended that the smaller the cut the hotter the temperature and the more quickly you should cook it; this is particularly true when cooking game. It is also important to remember that because game is high in protein it retains heat and continues to cook long after it has been removed from the heat source. So always make it hot and fast.

1 pound tenderloin
½ cup plus 3 tablespoons unsalted butter
2 tablespoons chopped parsley, preferably Italian parsley
Grated rind of 1 lemon

2 medium garlic cloves peeled, crushed or chopped fine
1½ cups stock (beef or chicken stock will do, veal stock is best)
6 crushed fennel seeds

Clean the venison tenderloin completely of all fat, silver-stein, etc. and rub with oil. In three tablespoons of hot butter sauté till brown on all sides and then continue to cook until done, approximately 10 minutes. Remove from the pan and let stand. Deglaze the pan with stock, adding the fennel seeds, lemon rind and garlic and reduce by half. Then lower the heat and whisk in the remaining butter. Season with salt and pepper. Slice the tenderloin in thin pieces, place on a serving platter or plates, and then add sauce, placing some under and atop the meat. (*Serves two*)

Peppered Roast of Venison

A simple roast recipe, but be certain to use a properly butchered and good cut of roast to ensure the nice venison taste.

4-5 pounds round of venison
1½ tablespoons lemon pepper
¾ teaspoon ground thyme
¾ teaspoon garlic salt

1 medium onion, thinly sliced
1 cup dry red wine
½ cup butter, melted

Wipe meat with a damp paper towel. Grind lemon pepper, garlic, salt and thyme with a mortar and pestle until well blended. Rub and pat onto all surfaces of the roast. Cover the roast with the onion slices, sticking a toothpick in each to hold it onto the venison. Roast 10 to 15 minutes per pound in a 350° oven. Baste the roast with a mixture of red wine and melted butter during the cooking. When done, remove and let stand for 15 minutes. Remove and discard the onion before carving. Serve with the pan juices. (*Serves eight*)

STEAKS & CHOPS

VENISON STRIP STEAK

Armagnac is a good substitute for cognac. Also a brandy, it's made in the French region of Gascony and tastes like cognac but often is a bit less expensive. This makes it perfect for deglazing unless your in an extravagant cognac sort of mood.

4 individual-size strip steaks (about ⅓ pound each)
2 tablespoons olive oil
¼ cup armagnac or cognac
½ cup veal stock

4 tablespoons unsalted butter
16 large capers
Salt and pepper

Pan-fry the steaks in oil a minute or two per side and remove to a plate. Deglaze the pan with with armagnac and add stock. Reduce the liquid to a quarter cup and whisk in the butter. Rinse the capers well and add to the sauce. Slice the steak, pour the excuding juices into the sauce and season with salt and pepper. Pour the sauce over the meat and serve. (*Serves four*)

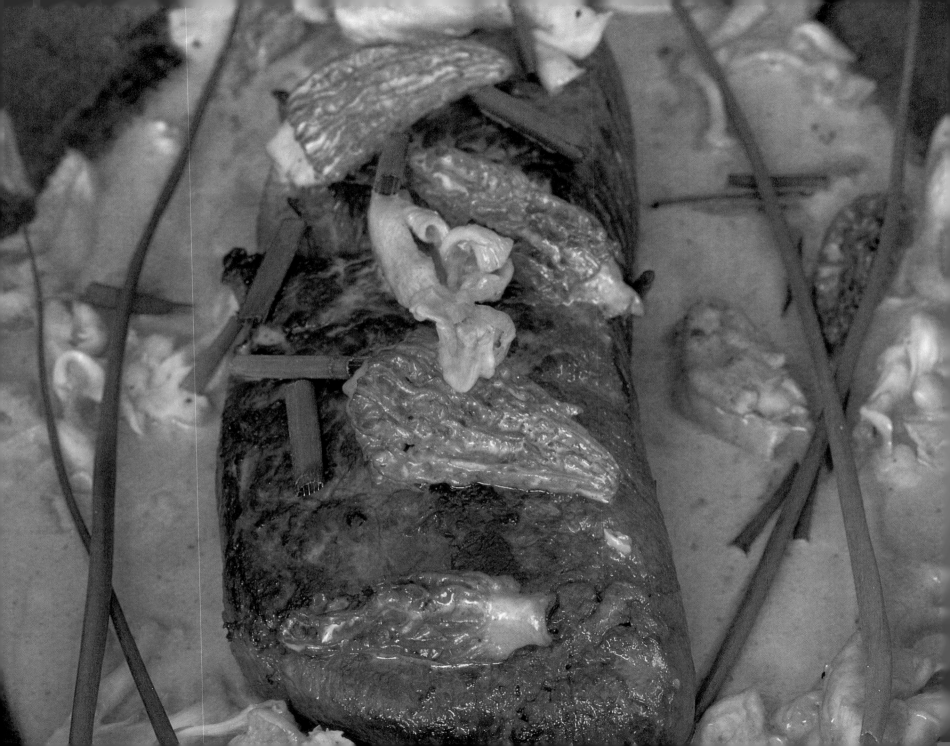

Venison Steak with Wild Mushrooms

When I first wrote this recipe in the 1980s it was very difficult to obtain fresh wild mushrooms; you were dependent on the season, wet weather and the expertise of an adventuresome fungophile. Today, with the ever-increasing cultivation of many wild mushrooms, a good grocery store often provides many of the exotics; and, of course, the dried varieties are very good, too.

2 pounds venison steak
1 tablespoon oil
¼ cup cognac or armagnac
1 ounce dried wild mushrooms (porcini are good)

1 cup heavy cream
⅓ cup veal or chicken stock
Salt and pepper

Soak the mushrooms in cold water for a minimum of 15 minutes. Remove and rinse the mushrooms, saving a bit of the water-bath. Add the mushrooms and a splash of the water-bath to a skillet along with the cream. Bring to a boil and then turn it down to a simmer until the cream is reduced by half. Pan-fry the steak in the olive oil, about four to five minutes on one side and three on the other. Make sure not to overcook. Remove the steak to a plate and deglaze the pan with the cognac and stock. Add the cream and mushroom mixture and any of the juices that have exuded from the steak and let simmer together for a few minutes. Season with salt and pepper and serve over the sliced meat. (*Serves four*)

Venison Steak Marinated

Juniper berries are one of my favorite spices to use in cooking all game; and although I give a quantity in each recipe, their wonderful aroma and gin flavor means there are almost never too many juniper berries in a recipe.

2 pounds venison steak
2½ cups olive oil
25-30 juniper berries, crushed and lightly chopped
Juice from 2 lemons (about ⅓ cup) plus the rind finely grated
1 teaspoon celery salt
10 peppercorns, crushed
2 tablespoons ground coriander seed

1 bay leaf, crumbled
2 tablespoons unsalted butter
¼ cup cognac
⅔ cup veal stock
½ cup heavy cream
2 teaspoons sour cream
Salt and pepper

In a blender, or with a mortar and pestle, blend the juniper berries, lemon rind, celery salt, peppercorns, coriander seed and bay leaf. Add this to the olive oil and lemon juice and marinate the steak at least overnight. Wipe the steak dry and pan-fry it in butter. Remove the meat from the pan and let it rest. Deglaze the pan with cognac and then add the veal stock. Bring to a boil and let reduce by a quarter. Add the heavy cream and let it boil and continue to reduce. Add any juices that have exuded from the steak while it has been resting and after it has been carved. Remove the sauce from the heat and whisk in salt and pepper and the sour cream. Serve over the meat. (*Serves four*)

POTTED VENISON STEAK

The purpose of a marinade is to tenderize the meat — which is specifically what the vinegar or wine does chemically — and a marinade can alter the flavor, too. You can substitute soy sauce for salt in any marinade recipe, and remember to never marinate meat in a metal container.

3 pounds venison steak
3 cups apple wine
2 teaspoons brown sugar
¼ teaspoon cinnamon
¼ teaspoon ginger
5 whole cloves

½ teaspoon salt
1 tablespoon cider vinegar
4 tablespoons butter
2 tablespoons flour
Tiny carrots, cooked, for garnish

Cut venison steak into six serving-size pieces and place in a glass or plastic pan in which the pieces fit nicely. Combine wine and sugar, seasonings and vinegar and bring to a boil. Pour over steaks and let marinate in the refrigerator for 24 hours.

When ready to cook, take the steak out of the marinade and pat dry with paper towel. Heat butter in a large skillet and brown meat on both sides. Add ½ cup of strained marinade and cook over a low heat for 30 minutes or until the venison is tender, adding more strained marinade as needed. When done remove the steaks to a platter and keep hot. Mix two tablespoons flour with one cup remaining strained marinade and add to skillet. Cook, scraping the brown bits from the bottom of the skillet, until mixture is thickened. Serve with the steaks and garnish the platter with the tiny carrots. (*Serves six*)

Venison Chops with Pignolis and Red Peppers

When I first wrote this recipe, flavored oils were all the rage, walnut oil being one of my favorites. Unfortunately, walnut oil, if not used often, can go rancid and is relatively high in saturated fat. Now with so many fine and tasty good, green olive oils available at grocery stores, it is perfectly acceptable to substitute the more prevalent and usable olive for walnut oil in this recipe if desired.

4 venison chops (1 per person)
¼ cup walnut oil
¼ cup pignolis (pine nuts)

2 tablespoons unsalted butter
1 sweet red pepper
Salt and pepper

Cut the red pepper and remove the seeds. Slice into thin strips and sauté in the butter. Sauté the pignolis separately in two tablespoons of the walnut oil. Toss the peppers and nuts together and set aside. Sauté the chops in the remaining walnut oil for a minute or two on each side. Place on plates and add the pepper-nut mixture to the top of each chop. Season with salt and pepper to taste. (*Serves four*)

Grilled Venison Chops with Blue Cheese and Caraway Seeds

Don't feel guilty about lathering lots of butter and cheese onto the chops here; the extreme leanness of venison meat affords us the great luxury of adding wonderful fat to the cooking process.

4 chops (I per person)
½ cup unsalted butter
I tablespoon blue cheese, crumbled
I teaspoon caraway seeds

Few drops of Worcestershire sauce
2 tablespoons oil
Salt and pepper

Whip the butter until soft. Add the cheese, caraway seeds, Worcestershire sauce and salt and pepper and mix well. Roll up in plastic wrap and shape into a log. Freeze for at least one hour or preferably overnight.

Pan-fry the chops in oil, two to three minutes per side (depending on thickness) and place on plates. Slice off two or three pats of the cheese-butter per chop and put on top to melt over the chops. (*Serves four*)

VENISON CHOPS

One of the great attributes of venison is that it is a very "light" meat, similar to veal or lamb. This makes it a near ideal breakfast meat.

4 venison chops
Olive oil, fine quality

4 eggs
salt and pepper to taste

Brush venison chops with olive oil and broil or grill on both sides for about five minutes total. Fry the eggs, sunny-side-up, and place atop the chops and serve. For a brunch you might want to add cooked asparagus and hollandaise sauce, layering the asparagus atop the eggs and chop and covering with the sauce. (*Serves four*)

Venison Chops with Mustard Butter

You may question the name of this recipe since butter is not included in the list of ingredients.
When heavy cream is "reduced" all of the water is evaporated and what remains is only the butter fat;
but I didn't think that a recipe entitled "Venison Chops With Mustard Butter Fat" sounded very appetizing.

4 venison chops
2 tablespoons oil
¼ cup cognac
¼ cup veal stock

½ cup heavy cream
1 tablespoon prepared coarse-grained mustard
Salt and pepper

Pan-fry the chops in oil and set a side. Deglaze the pan with cognac and add the veal stock and cream. Reduce to half the quantity, remove from the heat, and whisk in the mustard and any of the juices from the resting chops. Season to taste with salt and pepper and serve over the chops. (*Serves four*)

Charcoal Grilled Venison Steaks with Rosemary Butter

"Compound butters" are butter combined with various herbs, garlic, scallions and other flavorings.
They provide a handy method for adding tasty fat to lean meats, or for masking the flavor of those not-so-tasty fats such as in fish.
Compound butters are good to keep in the freezer for that instant touch of gourmet elegance.

2 pounds venison steak
½ cup unsalted butter
2 teaspoons dried rosemary

½ teaspoon minced garlic
Salt and pepper

Chop the rosemary very fine and crush a garlic clove or mince it fine. Whip the butter and add the rosemary, garlic and salt and pepper to taste. Wrap the butter in plastic wrap and shape into a log. Place in the freezer while you start the charcoal. Once the coals have burned down, but are still red-hot, cook the steak quickly, about four minutes per side depending on the steak's thickness. Cut slices of the butter to top each serving. (*Serves four*)

Venison Steak with Red Wine

I was taught to make and use veal stock in cooking school. It is time-consuming to make, but worth the effort.
It is best stored by freezing in ice trays; then keeping the veal cubes in a plastic freezer bag,
instantly ready to pop into the hot pot a cube or two at a time.

2 pounds venison steak
2 tablespoons olive oil
2 tablespoons finely chopped shallots
⅔ cup good red wine

½ cup veal stock
6 tablespoons unsalted butter
Salt and pepper

Pan-fry the steak in the olive oil until done, about four minutes per side depending on the thickness of the steak. Remove to a platter. In the pan put one tablespoon of butter and the shallots over medium heat and cook until they are just barely soft. Add the wine and bring to a boil, and continue boiling until you have a third left. Add the veal stock and simmer until you have about half a cup of liquid remaining. Slice the meat against the grain. Whisk in the remaining butter to the sauce and any of the juices from the steak on the platter. Season with salt and pepper and serve over the steak.

(*Serves four*)

Venison Chops with Basil Cream

This recipe has my favorite sauce to accompany venison: a bit of reduced cream. It's simple to do and the sweetness of the cream and basil are a lovely taste enhancement to the subtle but distinct flavor of the venison.

4 venison chops
1 tablespoon olive oil
1 tablespoon butter

1 pint heavy cream
1 tablespoon chopped, fresh basil (or ½ tablespoon dried)

Reduce the cream by pouring the cream into a frying pan, bring to a slow boil and add the basil. Simmer until thick and halved in quantity. If it gets too thick add a little water and stir. Meanwhile, cook the chops. Brush away any bone chips and remove any fat from the venison. In a frying pan with the hot oil and butter, sauté the chops very quickly, two to three minutes per side. The chops should be pink inside. In the pan add a little stock or water and deglaze; then add the basil cream. Whisk and season with salt and pepper and serve on top of the chops. (*Serves four*)

Venison Steak — London Broil Style

*Although this recipe calls for broiling the steak, it is also very delicious —
maybe even preferable if not too cold our rainy out — prepared on the grill.*

1 cup ale
½ cup olive oil
2 tablespoons lemon juice
1 garlic clove, crushed
½ teaspoon salt
1 bay leaf

Freshly ground pepper to taste
1 teaspoon prepared Dijon mustard
½ teaspoon dried rosemary
1 teaspoon fresh basil leaves, chopped fine (or ½ teaspoon dried)
2-3 sprigs fresh thyme (or ½ teaspoon dried)
1-2 pounds thick venison steak

Open ale and let stand at room temperature for several hours. Combine the ale, olive oil and seasonings. Put the steak in a flat pan and pour the oil mixture over it. Cover and let marinate overnight or at least eight hours, turning occasionally. Remove from marinade and broil, three inches from the heat source, for approximately six to seven minutes per side. Cool and then chill. Slice on the bias into very thin pieces and arrange on a platter. Serve with a cold béarnaise sauce (*see recipe on page 66*) or soy sauce with chopped scallions. (*Serves four*)

SUNDRY VERSATILES

Chateaubriand Butter with Venison Burger

In cooking school my teacher used to emphasize that it was often the simplest foods that were deceptively difficult to cook, example: a hamburger.
A result, I believe, of much of our hamburger being made from tasteless beef.
Assuredly by substituting venison burger, and adding some care to the cooking, these burgers will be wonderfully flavorful.

I cup white wine
3 shallots, chopped very fine
I handful of fresh parsley, chopped
I teaspoon chervil
I teaspoon tarragon

I cup chicken stock
I cup unsalted butter
2 pounds venison burger
Salt and pepper

In a small saucepan combine the wine, shallots, parsley, chervil, and tarragon and bring to a boil. Reduce heat and simmer very slowly until the liquid is reduced by half. Add the stock and continue to reduce until about half a cup of liquid is left. Whip the butter until soft and add the cooled wine and stock mixture. Season with salt and pepper and wrap in plastic wrap, shaping it into a log. Refrigerate at least one hour or overnight. Form venison burger into patties and cook rare over a charcoal grill. Slice several pats of the butter for each burger and serve on top. (*Serves eight*)

Venison Stew with Artichoke Hearts and Sun-dried Tomatoes

This is such an elegant dish that it deserves a better handle than stew or even goulash; perhaps "a medley of marvelous meat and venerable vegetables" would best describe. If you can find the tiny fresh artichokes (often in Italian markets) they can be cooked and used in the medley whole.

1½ pounds venison stew meat
4 tablespoons oil
1 small onion, chopped
1 small carrot, chopped
3 cups fine red wine
1 cup beef stock
Bouquet garni
½ cup sun-dried tomatoes

2 14-ounce cans (or 8 small fresh or 2 boxes frozen) artichoke hearts
1 tablespoon cornstarch (or arrowroot)
6 tablespoons butter
1 tablespoon chopped parsley
1 tablespoon grated lemon rind
1 clove garlic, chopped fine
Salt and pepper

Brown the meat in the oil and remove from the pan. Sauté the onion and carrot in the pan where the meat was. Return the meat to the pan and add the wine and stock to the pot. Bring to a boil and add the bouquet garni and the sun-dried tomatoes. Soak the canned artichoke hearts for a while in cold water to remove the brine taste (this is unnecessary if they are frozen). Or cook the fresh chokes in boiling water for 20 minutes, removing the hearts afterward. Add the artichokes to the pot. Cover the pot with foil, pressing down so there is no space between the foil and the liquid. Put the lid on and simmer for about 20 minutes or until a skewer comes out easily and cleanly from a piece of meat. When done, drain the juices into a frying pan and thicken with cornstarch. Whisk in the butter and season with salt and pepper. Return the seasoned butter to the meat and add parsley, garlic and lemon rind. Check for seasoning and serve. (*Serves eight*)

Venison Calzones

Generally served hot, venison calzones are also wonderful served cold, perhaps on a picnic, with a dollop of sour scream.

3 cups all-purpose flour
1 package (or 2 heaping teaspoons) yeast
1 teaspoon salt
2 tablespoons oregano
1 cup ground venison
2 tablespoons bacon fat

1 small onion, chopped fine
1 clove garlic, minced
½ cup slivered gruyere cheese
1 cup eggplant, cubed
2 tablespoons butter
Freshly ground pepper

In a medium bowl mix one cup of the flour with the yeast and add enough warm water (not hot) to make a moist, cohesive ball. Fill the bowl with warm water so the ball is covered. Let sit for 5 to 15 minutes until the ball pops to the surface. Meanwhile, take the remaining flour (this can be a mixture of two-thirds white and one-third whole wheat) and put it on top of the counter. Make a trench in the middle of the flour and add the salt. Reconstitute the oregano by adding a bit of hot water to it first and then add it to the trench. You may need to add more water so the mixture is cohesive but not wet. When the ball has risen to the surface scoop it out and set in the middle of the pile of flour. Knead the flour and the ball together for a minimum of eight min-utes. Put the dough in an oiled or floured bowl with a towel over it and set in a warm place for two hours or until it has doubled in size. Punch down then roll out into two squares measuring 8 x 8 inches.

Brown the burger along with the onion and garlic in the bacon fat. Then sauté the eggplant in butter. Put the burger, eggplant and cheese in layers in the center of the squares and season with pepper. Then pull a top corner of the dough over to meet the opposite bottom corner, forming a triangle, and pinch the seams together. Flip over so the seam is on the bottom. Let rise again for another 45 minutes and bake in a 425° oven till done (about 35 to 40 minutes). Slice each triangle in half and serve. (*Serves four*)

Venison Sausage

Grinding venison is not only time-consuming but difficult, unless you own a commercial and large-bladed meat-grinder.
If you can't find a butcher to grind the venison or purchase ground venison from any of the mail-order companies,
it's possible with this recipe to finely chop stew-meat venison and combine it with a high-percentage fat pork sausage.

2 pounds ground venison
2 pounds bulk sausage

¾ teaspoon salt
Freshly ground pepper

Be certain to use ground venison and pork sausage that has never been frozen. Combine all ingredients in a large mixing bowl and, preferably with your hands, mix together. Shape meat mixture into patties. Freeze what you don't intend to use right away. To cook, fry over medium heat for about 10 minutes, turning the patties to brown them. (*Serves eight*)

VENISON FONDUE

*If you were married in the 1960s obtaining a fondue pot should be only as difficult as going upstairs to the attic and rummaging among the other unused wedding gifts. Unless, of course, it has gone the way of many single-purpose and trendy appliances —
how about that stock-pot — and been lost to that garage sale back in the 1980s.
A good alternative to the fondue pot, and often more in keeping with the 1990s "open kitchen" eating environment,
is to keep a pot of hot oil on the stove at a low flame and let everyone grab a fork and cook their own pieces of meat right there.*

1 pound venison, cubed
Peanut oil

VARIOUS DIPPING SAUCES: Béarnaise, green may-
onnaise, honey mustard, barbecue, soy sauce, or
toasted sesame seeds

FOR A GOOD BÉARNAISE SAUCE:
¼ cup tarragon vinegar
2 tablespoons minced shallot
2 tablespoons minced fresh tarragon (or 2 teaspoons dried)
Dash of white pepper
3 egg yolks, lightly beaten
1 cup unsalted butter, melted
Salt
1 teaspoon chopped fresh cilantro

Combine the vinegar, shallot, tarragon and white pepper in a saucepan and simmer, reducing the mixture to about two tablespoons. Add a tablespoon of cold water and whisk in the three beaten egg yolks. Then, over very low heat and whisking all the while, dribble in the melted butter. Lift the pan occasionally if you need it to cool. Once the sauce has thickened add salt and more white pepper to taste and also the cilantro. Serve hot or chilled for the fondue. (*Serves four*)

Venison Black Bean Chili

If you've got boneless venison I can think of nothing finer than to have a pot of this elegant venison chili
simmering on the stove on a cold November day.

2 cups dried black beans (or 3 16-ounce cans)
¼ cup olive oil, approximately
1 stalk celery, chopped small
2 medium onions, chopped small
8 cloves garlic, chopped very fine
4 pounds boneless venison, cut in ½-inch cubes
1 teaspoon salt
3 tablespoons dried oregano
1 teaspoon cayenne pepper

½ teaspoon ground coriander
⅓ cup medium-hot chili powder
2 tablespoons ground cumin
3½ cups hot chicken stock (use Knorr chicken cubes)
28-ounce can Italian plum tomatoes
Approximately 8 cups cooked, short grain brown rice (or you can use
 wild rice if you are feeling lavish)
3-4 tablespoons chopped parsley for garnish
1 cup sour cream mixed with grated rind of 1 lemon, passed as garnish

Rinse the dried beans, remove any stones and cover with water in a large pot and bring to a boil. Remove from the heat, cover and let stand several hours. Then drain, cover with water again and cook for one to two hours until they are tender but still have some bite. (Some beans are tougher than others, and may need to be soaked overnight.) If using canned beans, just rinse well and drain. Heat half of the oil in a large cooking casserole and cook the celery and the onions over medium heat till soft, about 15 minutes. Add the garlic and cook another few minutes, stirring, then remove all from the pan to a small bowl. Heat the rest of the oil in the same pan, add the meat, stirring occasionally until the meat is gray — use medium heat; it should take no longer than 10 to 15 minutes. Then return the onion mixture to the pan and add salt, oregano, cayenne, coriander, chili powder and cumin. Mix and cook another 5 minutes. Now add the stock and canned tomatoes (break them with a fork) with their juices; bring to a boil. Stir well and simmer uncovered for two hours or until the meat is fork-tender. Stir in the beans and taste for seasoning. You may want more salt and oregano. Heat until hot and serve with rice, parsley and lemon sour cream. To thicken the juices, place a tablespoon or so of cornstarch in a glass and mix with a few tablespoons of water. Then add a few teaspoons of the hot chili liquid. Mix well, pour back into the pot and slowly bring to a boil stirring constantly — then remove from the heat. It should thicken right up. (*Serves eight*)

Venison Meat Pie

It is possible and nice to make the meat pie into four to six individual pies and then freeze them for a wonderful treat at a Saturday luncheon.

1½ pounds venison, cut into 1-inch cubes
½ cup flour
2 teaspoons salt
3 medium potatoes, peeled and sliced thin
1 large onion, sliced thin
¼ cup beef stock (or 1 can beef broth and ⅔ cup water)

FOR PASTRY:
2 cups sifted all-purpose flour
1 teaspoon salt
1 cup chilled butter
4-5 tablespoons ice water
1 egg yolk beaten with 1 tablespoon water

To make the pastry sift the flour and salt into a bowl and cut in the butter with a pastry blender until the texture of coarse meal. Sprinkle with ice water one tablespoon at a time, mixing with each addition until the consistency of dough. Wrap and chill in the refrigerator for at least one hour.

Divide the pastry in half and return one half to the refrigerator. Roll out pastry and line the bottom of the pie pan with it.

Dredge the meat in flour and salt. Layer potatoes and onions on top. Pour stock into the pie making sure that it doesn't overflow.

Remove the second half of the pastry from the refrigerator. Roll out and place on top of the filling. Trim the pastry even with the rim and crimp the edges. Brush with the egg-water mixture and slash each pie crust twice. Bake at 450° for 20 minutes, then reduce the heat and continue cooking at 350° for half an hour or until the meat is tender when you poke it with a skewer. (*Serves eight*)

Venison Loaf in Sour Cream Pastry

Although the addition of sour cream to the pastry dough gives it a very nice flavor, the practicality and ease of this dish
(and perhaps the quality, too, if your pastry has a tendency toward the gray and not-so-flaky) is greatly enhanced if you use ready-made pastry.
I recommend Pepperidge Farm's frozen flaky pastry sheets.

¼ cup butter
1 cup mushrooms, chopped fine
3 pounds ground venison
½ cup minced onion
⅓ cup parsley, chopped fine
1 cup grated Gruyere cheese
½ cup milk
Salt and pepper

FOR THE PASTRY:
2¼ cups all-purpose flour
1 teaspoon salt
¾ cup unsalted butter, chilled
2 eggs
½ cup sour cream or plain yogurt
2 tablespoons milk

For the pastry, sift flour and salt together into a large bowl. Slice the butter into ½-inch pieces and add to the flour, cutting in with a pastry blender until the mixture resembles coarse meal. Mix together one egg and the sour cream and stir into the flour mixture. Work dough until it leaves the sides of the bowl and becomes a soft ball. Wrap in wax paper and refrigerate for one hour.

To make the meat loaf, melt the butter in a skillet and sauté the mushrooms for about five minutes. Add the venison and cook, stirring occasionally, until brown. Remove from heat and stir in onions, parsley, cheese, salt and pepper and enough milk to moisten mixture and hold it together. Press into a loaf shape.

Cut the chilled dough in half and roll each half into rectangles that measure 6 x 14 inches, and cut off any excess scraps to be set aside for decoration. Place the meat loaf on one rectangle and cover with the second sheet of dough and press the edges together. Whisk together one egg and two tablespoons of milk and moisten the edges of the pastry with the milk mixture, crimping the edges with a fork. Decorate the loaf with the extra pieces of dough and brush with the egg-milk mixture. Prick the top of the loaf in several places with a fork to allow the steam to escape. Bake in a preheated oven at 375° for 45 minutes. Serve thick slices with a dollop of sour cream. (*Serves eight*)

VENISON SOUP

Venison, like most game, is a very rich and filling meat. And the portions and quantity of meat per serving that I've indicated in these recipes border on being gluttonous. Most chefs calculate about three ounces, or a quarter of a pound, of venison for each person. And, of course, for a soup it's whatever you have.

2 tablespoons butter
2 pounds venison, finely diced
1 large onion, chopped
2 leeks, sliced
2 Granny Smith apples, peeled and chopped
2-3 teaspoons curry powder

2 teaspoons salt
1 teaspoon sugar
3 quarts water
6 beef bouillon cubes
½ cup long-grain rice

Heat butter in a large soup pot. Add the venison cubes, onion, leeks, apples and cook, stirring until the venison is nicely brown and the vegetables soft. Stir in curry powder, salt and sugar. Then add the water, bouillon cubes and rice and simmer over low heat for two hours.

(*Serves fifteen*)

STIR-FRY VENISON

Stir-fry suits venison as it uses those sundry pieces of meat that seem to happen both when you trim a large purchased saddle, and too, when you do your own butchering.

½ cup red wine
½ cup beef broth
I teaspoon cornstarch
I tablespoon orange zest
I pound Asian egg noodles or angel-hair pasta
2 tablespoons peanut oil or wok oil

I pound venison cut into ¼-inch-thick strips
Salt and pepper
I garlic clove, crushed
I teaspoon freshly grated gingerroot
2 bell peppers, red and yellow, seeded and sliced
½ pound snow peas

Combine the wine, broth, cornstarch and orange zest in a small bowl and set aside. In a large kettle of boiling water cook the noodles according to the package directions. Drain well. While the noodles are cooking heat one tablespoon of the oil in a wok or heavy skillet until hot but not smoking. Stir-fry the venison strips quickly, seasoning with salt and pepper as you cook. Remove the meat to a plate and then add the other tablespoon of oil to the wok. Stir-fry the garlic, gingerroot, peppers and snow peas for about 30 seconds. Add the wine-broth mixture and simmer until the liquid begins to thicken; then add the cooked venison and any of the juices on the plate. Taste and correct seasoning. Toss with the noodles and serve. (*Serves four*)

Venison Shish Kebab

To simplify the cooking times, you may want to put all of the meat on one skewer, the mushrooms on another, the tomatoes on a third skewer and the zucchini on the fourth. Grill, cooking the meat a bit longer than the vegetables.

1-2 pounds venison, cut into large cubes
⅓ cup olive oil
½ cup red wine
1 garlic clove, crushed
Bouquet garni or your choice of herbs

½ pound cherry tomatoes
½ pound baby zucchini (or the larger ones cut into cubes)
½ pound portobello mushrooms
Salt and pepper
Skewers

Combine the oil, wine, garlic and bouquet garni in a bowl and marinade the venison cubes in the mixture for several hours. Clean and cut the mushrooms into large pieces about the same size as the meat. Skewer the venison pieces, alternating with the tomatoes, zucchini, and mushrooms. Season with salt and pepper. Grill on high heat and serve each skewer of venison and vegetables with rice. Or, pull meat and vegetables off the skewers and serve atop the rice. (*Serves six*)

SUPPLIERS

If you get venison from a wild source, you should know:

In the olden days (as in Robin Hood type old days) the word venison referred to any game, not just deer. I've not been quite that liberal with my use of the word, but in this book venison is used in its broadest sense to mean the deer family: caribou, moose, elk, antelope, white-tailed, red, fallow, and Sika deer. (This is a cook's taxonomy, I realize, and not a biologist's.) So all of the venison recipes in this book are applicable to these animals; making, of course the necessary quantity and cooking-time adjustments for the larger (or smaller) size of the various cuts.

If you need commercial sources for your venison, you should know:

Many, many grocery stores can now at least special-order venison on a week's notice; but should you need to mail-order your venison, listed below are several good sources. When trying to determine the portion size per person be aware that venison is very "rich" meat and quite filling. Most chefs estimate four ounces, or a third of a pound, of venison per serving. The recipes in this book are more generous, in general, with the suggested number of servings obtained per pound — predicting you and your guests are likely to want more of a great thing.

A.M. Briggs
2130 Queens Chapell Rd. NE
Washington, DC 20018
(202) 832-2600

Boyer Creek Ranch
Barronett, WI 54813
(715) 469-3394

Broken Arrow Ranch
P.O. Box 530
Ingram, TX 78025
(800) 962-4263

Czimer Foods, Inc.
13136 W. 159th St.
Lockport, IL 60441
(708) 301-7152

D' Artagnan, Inc.
280 Wilson Avenue
Newark, NJ 07105
(800) 327-8246 • (800) DARTAGN

Dole & Bailey Food Service
P.O. Box 2405
Woburn, MA 01888
(781) 935-1234

Farm Raised Foods
P.O. Box 696
Forest Lake, MN 55025-0696
(612) 464-6424

The Game Exchange
105 Quint St.
San Francisco, CA 94124
(415) 282-7878 • (800) GAME-USA

Game Sales International
P.O. Box 7719
2456 E. 13th St.
Loveland, CO 80537
(800) 729-2090

The Native Game Company
12556 Weld County Road 2½
Brighton, CO 80601
(800) 952-6321

Polarica Trading Corporation
105 Quint Street
San Francisco, CA 94124
(800) 426-3872

Rocky Mountains Natural Meats
6911 N. Washington
Denver, CO 80229

Venison America
Route 2, Box 2660
Elk Mound, WI 54739
(715) 874-6856

Venison World Inc.
Corner Hwy 83 & 87 • P.O. Box S
Eden, TX 76837
(800) 460-5326

Wild Game, Inc.
2315 W. Huron
Chicago, IL 60612
(800) 390-3663

Many thanks to D'Artagnan and Polarica Trading for supplying the

venison for all the photography in this book. It not only looks

good, it tasted great, too.

ADDITIONAL WILD GAME SUPPLIERS

Aidells Sausage Company
618 Coventry Road
Kensington, CA 94707
(415) 863-7485

American Ostrich Association
3840 Hulen Street, Suite 210
Fort Worth, TX 76107
(817) 731-8597

Aspen Gourmet
1654 Juniper Hill Road
Aspen, CO 81611
(800) 923-6033 • (970) 923-6033

Big Sky Buffalo
South Main Street • P.O. Box 224
Granville, ND 58741
(800) 570-7220

Chieftain Wild Rice Company
P.O. Box 550 • 1210 Basswood Avenue
Spooner, WI 54801
(800) 262-6368

Critchfield Meats
Zandale Shopping Center
2254 Nicholasville Road
Lexington, KY 40503
(800) 86MEATS • (800) 866-3287

Culver Duck Company
P.O. Box 910
Middlebury, IN 46540
(219) 825-9537

John Dewar
136 Market Square
Boston, MA 02118
(617) 442-4292

Foggy Ridge Gamebird Farm
Q13 Highland Road
Warren, ME 04864
(207) 273-2357

Galley Meats
610 S. Arroyo
Pasadena, CA 91101

Grimaude Farms
11665 N. Clements Road
Linden, CA 95236
(209) 887-3121

Jackson Hole Buffalo
(800) 543-6328

L.F.C.
3246 Garfield Street
Hollywood, Florida 33021
(954) 964-5861 • (888) EAT-GAME

Los Gatos Meats & Smoke House
575 University Ave.
Los Gatos, CA 95030
(408) 354-7055

MacFarlane Pheasant Farm, Inc.
2821 South U.S. Highway 51
Janesville, WI 53546
(608) 757-7881 • (800) 345-8348

Maison Glass
52 East 58th Street
New York, NY 10022
(212) 755-3316 • (800) 822-5564

Manchester Farms
P.O. Box 97
Daizell, SC 29040
(800) 845-0421

Mondo's & Sons
4225 Rainier Avenue South
Seattle, WA 98118
(206) 725-5433 • (206) 725-1565

National Bison Association
4701 Marion Street, Suite 301
Denver, CO 80216
(303) 292-2833

North American Deer Farmers Association
9301 Annapolis Road #206
Lanham, MD 20706-3115
301-459-7708

Old World Venison Co.
21654 100th Ave
Randall, MN 56475
(320) 749-2197

Ostrich Processing, Inc.
P.O. Box 2155
Thomasville, GA 31799
(800) 262-4737

Plantation Quail
1940 Highway 15 South
Greensboro, SC 30642
(800) 843-3204

Quail International, Inc.
(800) 843-3204

RC Western Meats
P.O. Box 4185
Rapid City, SD 57709
(605) 342-0322

Ranch House Meat Co.
P.O. Box 855
Menard, TX 76859
(800) 749-6329

S & B Farms
125 Lynch Road
Petaluma, CA 94954
(707) 763-4793

Santa Rosa Game Birds
1077 Butler Avenue
Santa Rosa, CA
(707) 546-1776

Sayersbrook Bison
6286 Spencer Road
Bonnettere, MO 63628
(573) 438-4449

Sonoma Foie Gras
P.O. Box 2007
Sonoma, CA 95476
(707) 938-1229 • (800) 427-4559

UnderHill Farms
187 21st Avenue
Moundridge, KS 67107
(316) 345-8415

Valley Game & Gourmet
615 West 100 South
Salt Lake City, UT 84104
(800) 521-2156

METRIC CONVERSIONS (APPROXIMATE)

LIQUID WEIGHTS

U. S. Measurements	Metric Equivalents
¼ teaspoon	1.23 ml
½ teaspoon	2.5 ml
¾ teaspoon	3.7 ml
1 teaspoon	5 ml
1 tablespoon (3 teaspoons)	15 ml
2 tablespoons (1 ounce)	30 ml
¼ cup	60 ml
⅓ cup	80 ml
½ cup	120 ml
⅔ cup	160 ml
¾ cup	180 ml
1 cup (8 ounces)	240 ml
2 cups (1 pint)	480 ml
3 cups	720 ml
4 cups (1 quart)	1 litre
4 quarts (1 gallon)	3¾ litres

DRY WEIGHTS

U. S. Measurements	Metric Equivalents
¼ ounce	7 grams
⅓ ounce	10 grams
½ ounce	14 grams
1 ounce	28 grams
1½ ounces	42 grams
1¾ ounces	50 grams
2 ounces	57 grams
3 ounces	85 grams
3½ ounces	100 grams
4 ounces (¼ pound)	114 grams
6 ounces	170 grams
8 ounces (½ pound)	227 grams
9 ounces	250 grams
16 ounces (1 pound)	464 grams

TEMPERATURES

Fahrenheit	Celsius (Centigrade)
32° F (freezing point)	0°C
200° F	95°C
212° F (boiling point)	100°C
250° F	120°C
275° F	135°C
300° F (low heat)	150°C
325° F	160°C
350° F (medium heat)	175°C
375° F	190°C
400° F (high heat)	205°C
425° F	220°C
450° F (very high heat)	230°C
475° F	245°C
500° F	260°C

LENGTH

U. S. Measurements	Metric Equivalents
⅛ inch	3 mm
¼ inch	6 mm
⅜ inch	1 cm
½ inch	1.2 cm
¾ inch	2.0 cm
1 inch	2.5 cm
1¼ inches	3.1 cm
1½ inches	3.7 cm
2 inches	5 cm
3 inches	7.5 cm
4 inches	10 cm
5 inches	12.5 cm

INDEX

ABOUT THE AUTHOR

Dubbed "Martha Stewart with a shotgun" by P.J. O'Rourke, Rebecca Gray has authored and compiled several cookbooks including the best-selling *Eat Like a Wild Man*. A contributing editor for *Sports Afield*, she also writes for such publications as *Cooking Light*, *Saveur*, and *Town & Country*. She lives in Lyme, New Hampshire.

ABOUT THE PHOTOGRAPHER

Photographer Christopher Hirsheimer is Executive Editor of *Saveur* magazine and has contributed photography to several cookbooks, including Julia Child's forthcoming book. She lives in Erwinna, Pennsylvania.

MELANIE ACEVEDO